D0597146

LIFE'S LITTLE
TREASURE BOOK

On
Simple
Pleasures

H. JACKSON BROWN, JR.

RUTLEDGE HILL PRESS®

NASHVILLE, TENNESSEE

Published in Nashville, Tennessee, by Rutledge Hill Press, Inc., 211 Seventh Avenue North, Nashville, Tennessee 37219.

Distributed in Canada by H.B. Fenn and Co., Ltd., 34 Nixon Road, Bolton, Ontario L7E 1W2. Distributed in Australia by The Five Mile Press Pty., Ltd., 22 Summit Road, Noble Park, Victoria 3174. Distributed in New Zealand by Southern Publishers Group, 22 Burleigh Street, Grafton, Auckland. Distributed in the United Kingdom by Verulam Publishing Ltd., 152a Park Street Lane, Park Street, St. Albans Hertfordshire AL2 2AU.

Typography by Compass Communications, Inc., Nashville, Tennessee

Illustrations by Jim Hsieh

Book design by Harriette Bateman

ISBN: 1-55853-746-5

Printed in Hong Kong

1 2 3 4 5 6 7 8 9 — 04 03 02 01 00 99

INTRODUCTION

When writing this little book, I was reminded once again of the joy and comfort that comes when we take time to experience life's simple pleasures. As we dash and crash, zig and zag our way through stressful schedules and impossible deadlines, we often forget that the satisfaction and fulfillment we seek can be found where we are and with what we already possess.

Dale Carnegie explained it this way: "Most are looking for some magical rose garden over the horizon instead of enjoying the roses blooming outside our windows." What we need is not more time and resources, but a new awareness and appreciation for the little priceless moments already ours to enjoy.

On the following pages you'll read some of the little things that have made a big difference in my life. I couldn't help but smile as I remembered each one:

- a congratulatory note from a friend
- mailing a college student a funny greeting card
- a neighbor's friendly wave
- freshly squeezed grapefruit juice
- homemade soup simmering on the stove
- leaving a quarter in the pay phone for the next person to find
- paying someone a compliment
- Junior Mints

Why not compile your own list? It's the best way I know of discovering that the little things we often take for granted aren't so little after all.

Living big and joyful and content is almost always the result of our finding satisfaction in life's ordinary day-to-day pleasures. And God must be fond of them too, for He made so many of them for us to enjoy.

$\mathcal{B}$less each day with your favorite music.

Blessed is the man who can enjoy the small things, the common beauties, the little day-to-day events: sunshine on the fields, birds on the bough, breakfast, dinner, supper, a friend passing by. So many people who go afield to search for happiness have left it behind them back home sitting on the front porch.

—David Grayson

Always have something beautiful in sight, even if it's just a daisy in a jelly glass.

Never regret any money spent on books or fresh flowers.

I've learned that . . .

. . . true serenity is holding your wife's hand when falling asleep at night. —Age 62

. . . beautiful flower gardens always seem to be tended by the nicest people. —Age 62

Simple Joys

- Grammar school Christmas pageants

- Stopping to read roadside historical markers

- Waking up to winter's first snowfall

- Homemade pumpkin bread, warm from the oven

*O*ften the deepest
relationships can be developed
during the simplest activities.

—Gary Smalley

❧

I think it ticks God off if you
pass the color purple in a field
somewhere and don't notice it.

—Alice Walker

$\mathcal{S}$urprise a loved one with a
little unexpected gift.

❧

$\mathcal{U}$se a picture of a loved one
as a bookmarker.

❧

$\mathcal{H}$old puppies, kittens, and
babies anytime you get
the chance.

*E*veryday happiness means getting up in the morning, and you can't wait to finish your breakfast. You can't wait to do your exercises. You can't wait to put on your clothes. You can't wait to get out—and you can't wait to get home, because the soup is hot.

—George Burns

Simple Joys

- Someone leaving the porch light on for you

- Music that makes you want to get down and boogie

- Sharing a funnel cake

- Taking a child to get her first library card

$\mathcal{I}$'ve learned that . .

. . . boredom is the result of not being aware of the beauty and the possibilities all around you.   —Age 73

. . . one of life's greatest joys is to have my two grand-children fight over my lap.

—Age 65

A contented mind is the greatest blessing a man can enjoy in this world.

—Joseph Addison

He is richest who is content with the least.

—Socrates

I still find each day too short for all the thoughts I want to think, all the walks I want to take, all the books I want to read, all the friends I want to see. The longer I live, the more my mind dwells upon the beauty and the wonder of the world.

—John Burroughs

Simple Joys

- Slow dancing cheek-to-cheek

- The smell of new-mown grass

- The song, "The Impossible Dream"

- Ranch dressing on almost anything

$\mathcal{S}$hare a box of animal crackers with a child.

✢

$\mathcal{L}$earn to play "Amazing Grace" on the piano.

✢

$\mathcal{P}$ut some little candy hearts on a loved one's pillow.

Simplicity is the key to seeing things clearly.

—Oswald Chambers

❧

The ordinary acts we practice every day at home are of more importance to the soul than their simplicity might suggest.

—Thomas Moore

$\mathcal{I}$ve learned that . . .

. . . you shouldn't wait until you are forty to get your first full body massage.

—Age 43

. . . my day is perfect when a song comes on the radio and my one-year-old wants to dance with me.

—Age 21

*Beauty of style and harmony
and grace and good rhythm
depend on simplicity.*

—Plato

∾

*Gratitude unlocks the fullness
of life. It turns what we have
into enough and more.*

—Melody Beattie

Simple Joys

- Cream of tomato soup and a grilled cheese sandwich

- Blowing someone a kiss

- The sound of my grandfather's voice saying grace

- A single magnolia blossom in a crystal bowl

*The foolish man seeks
happiness in the distance, the
wise grows it under his feet.*

—James Oppenheim

∾

*All you need for happiness is
a good gun, a good horse, and
a good wife.*

—Daniel Boone

*R*emember the three
universal healers:
calamine lotion,
warm oatmeal,
and hugs.

Simple Joys

- Snow geese flying in perfect formation

- Underwear still warm from the dryer

- An early morning walk on the beach

- Tootsie Roll Pops

$\mathcal{I}$ve learned that . . .

. . . watching a hummingbird build a nest, hatch, and care for her babies can brighten many days.

—Age 66

. . . nothing makes me feel better than talking to my sister over a pint of Ben and Jerry's.

—Age 15

We don't remember days, we
remember moments.

—Cesare Pauese

☙

$Smile$ at each other. Smile at
your wife, smile at your
husband, smile at your
children, it doesn't matter who
it is. And that will help you to
grow in greater love for
each other.

—Mother Teresa

Before we set our hearts too much upon anything, let us examine how happy they are who already possess it.

—François de La Rochefoucauld

❧

When you lose simplicity, you lose drama.

—Andrew Wyeth

Simple Joys

- Teaching a kid how to whistle

- Highway flagmen who wave

- A post card from a friend far away

- Overtipping a good waiter or waitress

One ought, every day at least, to hear a little song, read a good poem, see a fine picture, and if it were possible, to speak a few reasonable words.

—Johann Wolfgang von Goethe

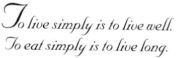

To live simply is to live well. To eat simply is to live long.

—Old English Proverb

I have learned, in whatever state I am, to be content.

—Philippians 4:11 (RSV)

My riches consist not in the extent of my possessions, but in the fewness of my wants.

—J. Brotherton

Simple Joys

- Easy-to-follow instruction manuals

- Repairmen who arrive on time

- Unexpected rainbows

- My mom's chicken pot pie

$\mathscr{I}$'ve learned that . . .

. . . leaving my seat and coming back to find it still warm always makes me happy.
—Age 26

. . . even the worst day can be improved with a kiss from a child.
—Age 32

Savor life's true delights—a crackling fire, a glorious sunset, a hug from a child, a walk with a loved one, a kiss behind the ear.

—John Anthony

To me a field of wildflowers is no more grand than a simple bouquet held close.

—Sallye Schumacher

$\mathcal{K}$eep a couple of your
favorite inspirational books
on your bedside table.

∽

$\mathcal{H}$ang a birdfeeder where
you can see it from your
kitchen window.

I exist as I am that is enough.
If no others in the world
be aware
Is it content
And if each and all be aware
Is it content.

—Walt Whitman

$\mathcal{W}$atch your children sleeping.

&

$\mathcal{K}$eep a special notebook.
Every night before going to
bed, write down something
beautiful you saw during
the day.

&

$\mathcal{V}$acuum while barefoot.

Simple Joys

- A collection of recipes in your grandmother's own hand

- Getting the perfect fortune in a fortune cookie

- The smell of Johnson's Baby Powder

- Truman Capote's *A Christmas Memory*

- Handmade Valentines

- Swinging as high as you dare in a playground swing

- A favorite pair of jeans

- Louis Armstrong singing "It's a Wonderful World"

$\mathcal{I}$'ve learned that . . .

. . . the more possessions I acquire, the less free I feel.

—Age 36

. . . one of life's simple pleasures is when you wake up at 3:00 in the morning and say to yourself, "Oh great, I've still got four more hours to sleep." —Age 20

Happiness is not a destination. It is found along the way in simple pleasures and in acts of kindness and love.

—HJB

∽

If the only prayer you say in your whole life is "thank you," that would suffice.

—Meister Eckhart

Simple Joys

- Campfire singalongs

- The scent of honeysuckle on a summer evening

- Pizza delivery service

- The enthusiastic way my dog always welcomes me home

A man is rich in the proportion of the number of things he can do without. Beware of all enterprises that require new clothes.

—Henry David Thoreau

∾

Everything should be as simple as possible, but no simpler.

—Albert Einstein

*D*raw from memory a sketch of your childhood bedroom.

❧

*M*emorize your favorite love poem.

❧

*V*olunteer to work a few hours each month in a soup kitchen.

Simple Joys

- Family touch football games

- Sipping hot chocolate in the bright sunshine on a winter day

- Big dogs with bandannas tied around their necks

- 4-H Club exhibits

One of the things I know about human nature is that all of us tend too put off living. We are all dreaming of some magical rose garden on the horizon—instead of enjoying the roses that are blooming outside our windows today.

—Dale Carnegie

I've learned that . . .

. . . nothing fills my heart
with joy like watching my
83-year-old grandpa work in
his garden.   —Age 27

. . . after I call the best friend
I had while growing up, I
smile all day.

—Age 54

Simple Joys

- Peach iced tea

- Learning something new

- The clear sound of wind chimes

- Inexpensive disposable cameras

- Braiding your daughter's hair

- Live piano music in a Nordstrom's Department Store

- Second-hand bookstores

- Anything a kid makes from popsicle sticks

In the end, what affects your
life most deeply are things too
simple to talk about.

—Nell Blaine

∞

There must be quite a few
things a hot bath won't cure,
but *I* don't know many of them.

—Sylvia Plath

When you find a coin on the ground, give it to the first person you see.

❧

Send your mom a thank-you card on your birthday.

❧

Take some silly photos of yourself and a friend in an instant photo booth.

It is the simple things of life that make living worthwhile, the sweet fundamental things such as love and duty, work and rest, and living close to nature.

—Laura Ingalls Wilder

$\mathcal{N}$ever buy a car without
a sunroof.

∾

$\mathcal{N}$ever pass up a chance to
be in a parade.

∾

$\mathcal{O}$rder a seed catalog and read
it on the first day of winter.

The moment one gives close attention to anything, even a blade of grass, it becomes a mysterious, awesome, indescribably magnificent world in itself.

—Henry Miller

∞

The most precious things in life are near at hand.

—John Burroughs

$\mathcal{I}$'ve learned that . . .

. . . doing something to brighten someone's day makes my day. —Age 23

. . . in the end it is the simple things we remember and cherish. —Age 85

Simple Joys

- The smell of wood smoke on a late fall evening

- The passenger in front of you on a long flight not reclining his seat

- Dual-control electric blankets

- Root beer in a frosty mug

In character, in manners, in style, in all things, the supreme excellence is simplicity.

—Henry Wadsworth Longfellow

∾

We gather simple pleasures like daisies by the way.

—Louisa May Alcott

$\mathcal{M}$ake some Rice Krispies squares and share them with a neighbor.

❦

$\mathcal{G}$o to the airport and watch friends and families greet deplaning loved ones.

❦

$\mathcal{P}$ut love notes in your child's lunch box.

$\mathscr{I}$'ve learned that . . .

. . . perpetual happiness equates to three things: good health, good friends, and good music. —Age 29

. . . a big hug from my husband can make all my problems go away. —Age 35

$Simplicity$ is the deepest
wisdom.

—Isaac Barrow

∾

All of the animals, excepting
man, know that the principal
business of life is to enjoy it.

—Samuel Butler

Simple Joys

- Opening a new can of tennis balls

- The fragrance of a gardenia bush in bloom

- Twins dressed alike

- The annual Thanksgiving dinner where the menu never changes

Even though you have ten thousand fields, you can eat no more than one measure of rice a day.

Even though your dwelling contains a hundred rooms, you can use but eight feet of space in a night.

—Chinese Proverb

The little things?
The little moments?
They aren't little.

—John Kabat-Zinn

No man can tell whether he is rich or poor by turning to his ledger. It is the heart that makes a man rich. He is rich according to what he is, not according to what he has.

—Henry Ward Beecher

Simple Joys

- Hot oatmeal sweetened with real maple syrup

- Marking the last item off of a to-do list

- The striking of a grandfather clock

- The romantic inscription inside a wedding band

One can get as much exultation in losing oneself in a little thing as in a big thing. It is nice to think how one can be recklessly lost in a daisy.

—Anne Morrow Lindbergh

$\mathcal{I}$'ve learned that . . .

. . . no matter how much fun you had on vacation, the best part is coming home and sleeping in your own bed.

—Age 15

. . . there is no greater feeling than hearing for the first time, "I love you, Grandma."

—Age 56

I'd rather have roses on my table than diamonds on my neck.

—Emma Goldman

Much happiness is overlooked because it doesn't cost anything.

—William Ogden

∾

Each day as I look at the wonder of the world, I wonder where my eyes were yesterday.

—Bernard Berenson

$\mathcal{N}$ever miss an opportunity
to sleep on a screened porch.

∾

$\mathcal{N}$ever miss an opportunity
to ride on a roller coaster.

∾

$\mathcal{N}$ever refuse a holiday
dessert.

It isn't the big
pleasures that count
the most; it's making
a great deal of the
little ones.

—John Webster

One of the hardest lessons we have to learn in this life, and one that many persons never learn, is to see the divine, the celestial, the pure in the common, the near-at-hand— to see that heaven lies about us here in this world.

—John Burroughs

Simple Joys

- A bubble bath illuminated by vanilla-scented candles

- Browsing through an old hardware store

- Writing "Wash Me" with your finger on the back window of someone's car

- *Sesame Street's* Bert and Ernie

$\mathscr{I}$'ve learned that . . .

. . . nothing makes my day
like finding a parking space
just when I need it.   —Age 43

. . . my daddy is the wealthi-
est man in the world because
he believes that Mom and us
kids make him so.

—Age 19

When we forget the obvious, the little joys, the meals together, the birthday celebrations, the weeping together in time of pain, the wonder of a sunset or of a daffodil peeping through the snow, we become less human.

—Madeleine L'Engle

Simple Joys

- A cat that comes when you call it

- The TV character Fred Mertz on *I Love Lucy*

- Naming your new puppy

- Flea market browsing with a best friend

- Awaking to the smell of coffee brewing and bacon frying

- The first day of the year warm enough to wear shorts

- Giving a big smile to the greeter at Wal-Mart

- Bathroom air fresheners

$\mathcal{I}$t is good to be able to get excited over life's simple things. Unlike the big things, they are abundant and available to us twenty-four hours a day.

—HJB

I've learned that . . .

. . . the thing that goes the farthest toward making life worthwhile that's worth the most and costs the least is just a friendly smile. —Age 81

. . . in life, most good things come unexpectedly. —Age 13

Year by year the complexities of this world grow more bewildering, and so each year we need all the more to see peace and comfort in joyful simplicities.

—Woman's Home Companion
December 1935

Life's sweetest joys are hidden in unsubstantial things.

—May Riley Smith

. . . clocks ticking . . . and Mama's sunflowers. And food and coffee. And new-ironed dresses and hot baths . . . and sleeping and waking up. Oh, earth, you're too wonderful for anybody to realize you.

—Thornton Wilder, *Our Town*

The most beautiful sight you will ever see is your child running to you with outstretched arms.

—HJB

∽

I got a huge check and on the same day I got a huge kiss and hug from my child. The kiss and the hug felt better.

—Gary Fenchuk

*J*oys come from simple and natural things: mists over meadows, sunlight on leaves, the path of the moon over water.

—Sigurd Olson

I believe the nicest and sweetest days are not those on which anything very splendid or wonderful or exciting happens, but just those days that bring simple little pleasures, following one another softly, little pearls slipping off of a string.

—Lucy Maud Montgomery

The best and most beautiful things in the world cannot be seen or even touched. They must be felt with the heart.

—Helen Keller

*R*emember that all
important truths
are simple.

Dear Reader,

If you would like to share one of your favorite simple joys or simple pleasures with me, I would love to hear from you. My address is:

H. Jackson Brown, Jr.
P.O. Box 150014
Nashville, TN 37215

On the Web:
www.instructionbook.com
e-mail: llpio@aol.com